# HAUNTED
# HOUSES

Rev. R. W. and Mrs. Hardy

detail of the Tulip Staircase photograph shown on page 54

# HAUNTED HOUSES

written and illustrated by
## LARRY KETTELKAMP

Xerox Education Publications

XEROX

## By the Same Author

DREAMS

DRUMS, RATTLES, AND BELLS

FLUTES, WHISTLES, AND REEDS

GLIDERS

HORNS

KITES

MAGIC MADE EASY

THE MAGIC OF SOUND

PUZZLE PATTERNS

SHADOWS

SINGING STRINGS

SONG, SPEECH, AND VENTRILOQUISM

SPINNING TOPS

SPOOKY MAGIC

Library of Congress Catalog Card Number 69-14269
        3  4  5  6  /  76  75  74
Xerox Education Publications paperback edition
published by arrangement with William Morrow and Company.

XEROX® is a trademark of XEROX CORPORATION

The author wishes to thank
the following researchers for contributing materials
and offering helpful suggestions:

Dr. Stanley Krippner, Director
William C. Menninger Dream Laboratory
Department of Psychiatry
Maimonides Medical Center
Brooklyn, New York

Mr. William Cox
Foundation for Research on the Nature of Man
Institute for Parapsychology
Durham, North Carolina

Mr. William Roll, Project Director
Psychical Research Foundation, Inc.
Durham, North Carolina

Dr. Thelma Moss
The Neuropsychiatric Institute
U.C.L.A. Center for the Health Sciences
Los Angeles, California

Dr. Gertrude Schmeidler
Department of Psychology
The City College of the City University of New York

# CONTENTS

# INTRODUCTION

Have you ever seen a ghost? Is there really such a thing? Are haunted houses just the product of superstition and imagination? People have always been interested in ghosts, and today we still are trying to find out what they are.

A ghost may be defined as the "spirit" of a

person who is no longer living. A ghost is usually a stranger to the person who sees it. When the same ghost is seen over and over again by one or more people in the same location, it is called a haunt, an expression which comes from a word meaning *home*. In most cases ghosts seem to haunt houses or buildings where they once actually lived. Reports of haunts sometimes continue off and on over a period of many years. Several sets of occupants of a particular house may all give somewhat similar reports even though they may not have heard about the ghosts before they saw them.

A special kind of ghost is the one called the poltergeist. The name comes from a German word that means "noisy ghost." Poltergeist cases are also associated with particular houses. Usually a poltergeist case lasts only a few days or weeks, but during this time the house may be made very difficult to live in. Objects seem to move or throw themselves about. Furniture may tip over. Dishes may break and liquids spill. Sometimes the movements occur in rooms where no people are present. At other times they may happen before the eyes of family members, friends, or investigators. Knocks, raps, thumps, or explosive sounds usually accompany the strange happenings, so the name poltergeist is very descriptive. Poltergeist effects are thought to be caused in some way by a member of the household; the phenomena might be called "spirits of the living."

Sometimes hauntings and poltergeist effects seem to be combined, making a very lively house indeed!

In the pages that follow you will read about a number of the best-known haunted houses, some from the past and some very recent. And you will learn of the intriguing theories suggested to explain them. Perhaps you will have some theories of your own as well about how these strange events can happen.

# SOME
# FAMOUS
# GHOSTS

## THE TOWER OF LONDON

It was the year 1864. A uniformed guard was
standing at his post before a door in the famous
Tower of London. He was a member of the
60th Rifles, the British guards quartered in
the Tower. Suddenly the figure of a woman in

white moved toward the guard. He called out a challenge, but the woman paid no attention. The guard charged with his pikestaff, which went right through the figure as if nothing were there! He was so surprised that he fainted and was found later by the other guards. The authorities thought that he had fallen asleep at his post, and he was given a trial by court martial.

At the trial the guard described the details of what had happened to him. The chances are that he would not have been believed. But fortunately an officer had seen the entire scene. He was Major General Dundas, who happened to be looking out of a Tower window just as the figure of the woman appeared below. His account of the incident agreed in every detail with the guard's and the man was acquitted.

During the testimony at the trial it was revealed that the figure the soldiers had seen was believed by many to be the ghost of Anne Boleyn, one of the famous wives of King Henry

VIII. Above the door at the guard's post was the room where Anne Boleyn had spent the last days before her execution.

No more likely place for legends and reports of ghosts could exist than the fortresslike group of walls and buildings called the Tower of London. The Tower is close to 900 years old. It has been used as a fortress, a weapons arsenal, a home for royalty, a prison, an observatory, and is now a tourist attraction. The Tower is best known as the place where a whole series of royal personalities were murdered or executed. There is a story that the young sons of King Edward IV were ordered murdered in the Tower by Richard III so that he could gain the throne. Sir Thomas More, Lady Jane Grey, the Earl of Essex, and the Duke of Monmouth were all killed there. And two of the wives of Henry VIII were executed in the Tower—Anne Boleyn in 1536 and Katherine Howard in 1542.

Shortly before Katherine's death when she was imprisoned in the Tower, she escaped from her room and ran down a gallery to the door of

Anne Boleyn

Katherine Howard

the Chapel of St. Peter. She cried out but the
king, who was inside the chapel, paid no attention. The guards carried her back to her
room and soon after, she was executed.

Katherine Howard seems to return to the Tower as a ghost to run again down what is now called the haunted gallery to the chapel crying for help. On two separate occasions, a year apart, witnesses reported hearing screams coming from the gallery. Other reports include a description of a woman with a desperate and hopeless expression running back from the chapel along the gallery until she disappears through the closed door at the end.

The ghosts seen in the Tower are typical of the ghosts of people who have died in tragic circumstances. In some automatic way they, or some form of their memories, seem still to be attached to the scene of the tragedy.

## THE HAUNTED RECTORY

One of the most famous haunting and poltergeist cases of all time is that of Borley Rectory. Borley was built by the Reverend Henry Martin in 1865, about sixty miles outside London. A succession of clergymen and their families who lived there reported strange happenings. Some who might have remained longer left after only a brief stay, unable to cope with the place. Many of the incidents at the rectory seemed to involve a mysterious nun.

In July, 1900, three sisters of the Reverend Harry Bull came back to Borley from a garden party. Just as they entered the grounds of the rectory, they saw a nun with her head bowed, her beads in her hand. She seemed to both slide and walk along the lawn. One of the sisters went to get a fourth sister, and they all stood watching the nun. The last sister, Elsie, started to go up to her. The nun turned and looked at them with an expression of great sadness—and then quickly vanished. All four sisters could see the nun very clearly. An investigator later interviewed three of the sisters, each one alone. Their descriptions of the event matched in every detail.

Another report of the nun was made by a carpenter named Fred Cartwright. He had been hired to repair some farm buildings not far from the rectory. On his way to work he walked past the house early each morning for several days. The morning of the second day, a Tuesday, he noticed the nun outside. On Friday he saw her again at the same time and place. He thought she looked tired. The next Wednesday she was there again just as he passed. This time he paused and turned to speak to her, but she had disappeared. The carpenter thought she must have gone inside. He did not know that no one was living in the rectory at that time, and so he was not suspicious. On Friday she was outside again, and this time he approached her directly to say good morning— but in a moment she was gone. Only later did the surprised carpenter hear about the accounts of the nun's ghost from others in the neighborhood.

A third report recorded by Harry Price in a book he wrote about Borley Rectory was that of an employee named Cooper. Edward Cooper and his wife lived in a cottage near the rectory for about three years, beginning in April, 1916. During this period they had many strange experiences there. Almost every night they could hear what sounded like a dog pattering around, but when they investigated, no dog could be found. One night when Mr. Cooper was getting ready for bed, he happened to look out the window. There was a moon and the night was clear. He noticed lights coming rapidly toward the cottage across the meadow near the rectory. Harry Price described the event.

"Wondering what the lights were doing in the Church meadow opposite, he gazed in astonishment as he realized that they were the headlamps of an old-fashioned black coach drawn by two horses. On the box seat were two figures in high top-hats. The metal trap-

pings of the horses glittered in the moonlight,
and everything was perfectly visible. The coach
swept on, through the hedge, across the road,
and into the rectory farmyard, where it disappeared. It was quite noiseless, and passed
*through* all obstacles."

At other times witnesses heard hoofbeats,
and the coach was also seen from various

angles. Once Mr. Bull heard the hoofs and wheels pass by him as he entered one of the driveway gates. This time he saw nothing. There were other reports of the sounds alone.

Noises in the house and movements of objects also were often reported at Borley. The poltergeist effects seemed most frequent during the time when children were living with their families in the house. In 1930, a Mr. Morrison, a minister, with his wife, Marianne, and their twelve-year-old daughter moved into the rectory for a period of five years. Both Mr. and Mrs. Morrison heard a voice calling, "Marianne," as if to get Mrs. Morrison's attention. Mrs. Morrison was struck several times by objects that were invisibly thrown in her direction. And messages began to appear by themselves on the walls. Again they seemed designed to attract the attention of Mrs. Morrison. They were short, halting phrases like, "Marianne—please—get—help."

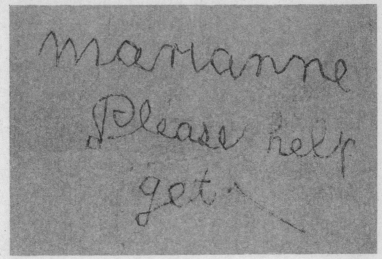

from a photograph of one of the
wall messages at Borley Rectory

Harry Price was invited to the rectory for
further investigation of the new happenings.
Later, after the Morrisons finally moved out,
the house was put up for sale. However, nobody wanted to buy such a weird residence.
Finally, in 1937, Mr. Price arranged to rent
the rectory as a kind of laboratory for investigators. For a year a whole group of researchers
took turns living in the house, several at a time.
The group included psychical investigators,

students, and others interested in probing the mysterious events. During this period many new messages for Marianne appeared on the walls. As a fresh message was noticed, it would be circled and dated. Some of the messages for help appeared before the eyes of the investigators. One such example was witnessed by Professor Joad, a philosopher and psychologist from the University of London. The nun was also seen several times during this year-long investigation.

It is a familiar phenomenon that haunted houses feel cold or chilly at times. Two cold spots were discovered in Borley. The researchers recorded the temperature in these two locations and found that it stayed at about a constant forty-eight degrees Fahrenheit, no matter how high the temperature was in the rest of the house. Even on a hot day the cold spots stayed cold.

In 1939 Borley Rectory was destroyed by

fire. Gradually what was left of the walls and floors crumbled and fell. Still interested in the case, Harry Price had the ruins excavated in an effort to find more clues to the strange puzzle. Many of the reports suggested that the nun may have been the one who in a mysterious way had been asking for help. Materials, including part of a skull and some human bones, which might bear out this theory, were found under the cellar floor. A scientist identified the skull as that of a woman, using archeological techniques considered sound and objective. Whether or not the skull was actually that of the nun could not be determined.

Although Borley Rectory is gone, the case remains one of the most interesting in the history of psychical research.

## THE MANOR HOUSE GHOST
In 1964 the cameras of the National Broadcasting Company were taken to England to at-

tempt the filming of a TV special on famous haunted houses. The name of the program, "The Stately Ghosts of England," was based on the name of a book that had been written about the houses. One of the most interesting old homes was the manor house called Longleat. The television team interviewed people who had seen or heard ghosts in the house. They also tried to photograph the locations where the ghosts had been reported, with some strange results.

The Marquess of Bath, whose ancestors had lived in the house, gave the account of a ghost called the Green Lady. A family portrait of her shows a lady in a green gown. Her name was Lady Louisa Carteret, and one of Lord Bath's ancestors had married her in 1735. However, the marriage did not go well. Lady Louisa met a young man at a dance given at Longleat and fell in love with him. In a hall on the third floor of the house Louisa's husband fought a duel with her lover and killed him. Within a short time Lady Louisa herself died of a broken heart. The third-floor hall where the duel occurred is the place where strange things have been noticed. Servants in the house will go out of their way to avoid walking through this section.

The NBC crew set up cameras to photograph the third-floor area. From the very beginning they had mysterious problems. Roll after roll of color film was developed and showed nothing at all but yellowish or greenish haze. New cameras were brought in, and new film stock was tried with no better results.

Automatic equipment had been set up to shoot film footage during the night. It would be found inexplicably shut off the following morning. The tapes from tape recorders were as bad as the muddy films. Unusual accidents began to occur. By itself a reflector floodlight rolled out of a bedroom, down a hall, hit a banister, then fell over it to crash down the open stair-

well. It almost hit an NBC crew member. Other lights blew up, and telephones went dead. It was reported that during an attempt to film a grandfather clock striking midnight, every other clock in the house struck the hour except the one that was being photographed. A crew member made some sharp remarks about the clock, and the next day he had an automobile accident.

Finally the film director tried a new approach. As strange as he felt about it, he walked into the third-floor hall and said to the ghosts, "I believe you are doing this. If you want me to ask your permission, I do humbly ask that you permit us to put this story on film." After that the trouble stopped. And a special camera on the third floor filmed a most unusual sequence. This camera had been set to take shots automatically at intervals during the night. When the time-lapse shots were developed, there was a sequence in slow motion. It showed a light like an automobile headlight coming out one door, moving down the hall, and then disappearing behind another door.

Nobody could figure out any logical explanation for the light.

The rest of the filming was completed without any unusual difficulty. The TV special, "The Stately Ghosts of England," complete with the movie of the mysterious moving light was broadcast on January 25, 1965.

## THE CALIFORNIA GHOST

Joe Hyams, a reporter, and his actress wife, Elke Sommer, moved into a two-story house in Beverly Hills, California, in July of 1964. Only a few days later the first of a series of reports of a ghost began. Mr. Hyams was not home and his wife had invited a guest for tea during the afternoon. As the guest, a journalist, described the incident to an investigator later, she saw a man come out to the area of the swimming pool where she was visiting. He walked quickly around the pool and seemed

to be looking intently at something. She described him as being middle aged with a "potato nose." He was dressed in a black suit with white shirt and tie. The guest was puzzled because she had not been introduced to the man. When she glanced toward him a second time, he was no longer there. She asked what had become of the man, but nobody knew whom she was talking about.

A similar experience was related about two weeks later by a man who was cleaning the swimming pool. He had been told that the house would be empty that day, since the owners were away. Therefore, he was surprised when he glanced in the window and saw a man walking quickly toward the dining room with his hands behind his back. He described him as an older, heavyset man with graying hair, wearing dark trousers and a white shirt and tie. The maintenance man went into the house to see who was there, but could not find a trace of the man he had seen through the window.

Mr. Hyams wrote an article for the *Saturday Evening Post* relating the series of strange events in the house. He and his wife noticed unusual noises coming from the dining room at night, like the sound of chairs being pushed back from the table. But every time they checked, the chairs were all in place. During August Mr. Hyams happened to be staying home alone for a few weeks, and he had the strange feeling that someone was there with him. Each morning a particular downstairs bedroom window that had been shut and locked the night before was found open. The front door was heard to open and shut twice, but no one was there. And the sounds of chairs being pushed back from the table in the dining room continued.

In an attempt to solve the problem, Mr. Hyams bought three miniature radio transmitters and three F.M. radios to pick up the signals. He also purchased three tape recorders, one for each radio. He placed one microphone near a driveway entrance, another at the front door, and a third one on the bar in the dining room. The equipment was turned on that night so that any sounds would be broadcast upstairs to the radios in the bedroom. At the same time they would be recorded on the tape machines. The noise of the chairs moving below was heard again, this time clearly over the broadcast system. Mr. Hyams went downstairs with a pistol. When he switched on the dining-room light the sounds stopped. All the chairs were in place. The positions of the legs had been marked on the floor earlier with chalk, and nothing had been moved. When the tape was played back later the entire sequence was there. First the sounds of the chairs moving, then these sounds stopping as the click of the light switch was heard. The tape also picked up the noise of Mr. Hyams coughing while he was in the dining room; then after he had left the room the tape picked up still more sounds of chairs moving!

A friend of Mr. Hyams', who had not been told about the ghost, stayed in the house while his own was being redecorated and the Hyams were away. The friend wrote to Mr. Hyams giving his own report of the same noises and the strange opening of the same downstairs window. Mr. Hyams had hired a detective to watch the house while he was away, and the detective reported seeing all the lights go on at once when no one was home.

The strange events and reports continued. Altogether four people witnessed an unknown man moving around in the house. These reports were separated by varying periods of time.

Information about the case reached the Neuropsychiatric Institute at U.C.L.A. Dr. Constas and Dr. Gorney of the institute arranged for an investigation of the case. Dr.

Thelma Moss, a co-worker, and Dr. Gertrude Schmeidler, a psychologist at the City College in New York, worked together on a plan. Dr. Schmeidler had tried a new method of investigation with another haunted house, and Dr. Moss decided to follow a similar idea.

The plan was carried out with the cooperation of members of the American Society for Psychical Research. Dr. Moss and Dr. Schmeidler did not actually go to the house. In this way they hoped to be able to report the results more objectively.

The Hyams were anxious for a solution to the problem and gave full cooperation to the scientists. First the A.S.P.R. members interviewed separately each of the four people who had seen the strange man. Their descriptions were somewhat similar.

Dr. Moss made up a list of words that described a variety of physical appearances and personality traits. Within this list were scattered the words the four witnesses had used to describe the man and his personality. Also a diagram was drawn up of the room plan of each floor of the house and the surrounding grounds.

Sixteen people were chosen to fill out a form choosing the words that best described the ghost of the man, and those words that were most unlike the man. They were also asked to check the places on the house plans where the ghost might have been seen.

Eight of these people were chosen as what are called "control subjects." They had never been to the house and knew nothing about it. They were simply told that a male ghost had been reported at the house. Each control subject was taken through the house by an A.S.P.R. member, and asked to fill out the forms as if he could imagine seeing a male ghost there.

The second group of eight people had one quality in common. They were all reported to have unusual psychic abilities. They could at times give accurate information about people whom they did not know, suggest events that might actually occur later, or relate accurate information that they felt came from persons who were no longer living. These individuals, who seem to be in contact with a world unknown to most people, are psychics.

The eight sensitives were taken separately to the Hyams house by an A.S.P.R. worker. They had been told nothing about the details of the reports of the ghost. Each sensitive was free to walk anywhere in the house or on the grounds and to form impressions of what the ghost might have been like and where it might have appeared. On their individual excursions, each sensitive described some perception of a personality. One reported seeing a girl near the pool, when there was no one there. The other sensitives gave various descriptions of a man, specifying his personality and activity. In addition to the eight control subjects and the eight sensitives, the forms were also given to the four eyewitnesses to fill out.

Then all of the forms were compared. As was expected, the descriptions given by the control subjects had little in common with the descriptions given by the four witnesses. Of the forms submitted by the eight sensitives, two were not used because they were not filled out correctly. Of the forms submitted by the other six sensitives, only three showed a high similarity to those of the witnesses. Even among the witnesses some of the descriptions did not agree. But there was enough agreement between the three sensitives and some of the witnesses' checklists to show that at least these three sensitives had sensed a ghost much like the man who had been reported earlier.

It turned out that the description of the girl seen by the pool fitted that of a girl whom Mrs. Hyams had known in Europe, who had died recently. In some ways the ghost of the man was like a doctor with whom Mr. Hyams had done some work, and who had recently died. The ghost also seemed somewhat like Mrs. Hyams' father, who had died some time earlier.

During the course of the investigation one of the sensitives reported her impressions that there was going to be a fire in the house, possibly in about six months but not necessarily that soon. She thought that it would be raining when the fire broke out. She also predicted that Mr. and Mrs. Hyams would move out of the house within two years.

Early in the morning of March 13, 1967, during an unusual California rainstorm, fire did break out in the Hyams' house. Mr. and Mrs. Hyams were awakened by loud pounding on the bedroom door. When Mr. Hyams opened it, there was nothing but smoke. He and his wife crawled out of a window to safety. They later found out that the fire had started in the mysterious dining room.

True to the prediction, Mr. and Mrs. Hyams moved out of the house and put it up for sale. The mystery of the ghost, the fire, and the warning pounding on the bedroom door were left behind.

## THE GHOST IN THE MUSIC BUILDING

An unusual ghost experience was reported by Coleen Buterbaugh, a secretary at Wesleyan University in Lincoln, Nebraska. Mrs. Buterbaugh reported the experience to a leading American psychologist and psychical researcher, Dr. Gardner Murphy. In order to bring back more of the details Mrs. Buterbaugh was hypnotized and asked to remember the experience as it had happened.

On an October day in 1963 Mrs. Buterbaugh walked into a university building where students were practicing music. It was ten minutes before nine in the morning, and she was on her way to deliver a message to an office in the building. She could hear students playing music in the practice rooms as she walked down the hall. She turned into the office and had taken just a few steps when a very strong disagreeable odor made her stop. At the same time all of the sounds in the building stopped. Mrs. Buterbaugh looked up and saw a tall woman reaching for some music on a high shelf in the room. She wore a long-sleeved white blouse and a long dark skirt. She had a bushy hairdo and looked like someone dressed in the costume of an earlier time in history.

Mrs. Buterbaugh described her experience in these words, "I looked up and there she was. She had her back to me, reaching up into one of the shelves of the cabinet with her right hand, and standing perfectly still. She wasn't at all aware of my presence. While I watched her she never moved. She was not transparent and yet I knew she wasn't real. While I was looking at her she just faded away—not parts of her body one at a time, but her whole body all at once."

"While I was looking at her she just faded away...."

Mrs. Buterbaugh also felt the presence of a person seated at a desk in the room, but could see no one. Then she looked up to the window behind the desk. What she saw frightened her and she described it with these words, ". . . it was then, when I looked out the window behind that desk that I got frightened and left the room. I am not sure whether I ran or walked out of the room . . . when I looked out that window there wasn't one modern thing out there. The street was not even there and neither was the new Willard House. That was when I realized that these people were not in my time, but that I was back in their time."

Mrs. Buterbaugh had seen the open fields which had been outside the building before the university had grown to its present size. As she quickly left the room and went back into the hall, she again heard the sounds of students practicing music.

In the university files a photograph was

found that showed the campus as Mrs. Buterbaugh had seen it. The photograph had been
taken in 1915. In some old yearbooks the
picture of a music teacher was found who
looked like the tall woman Mrs. Buterbaugh
had seen. She had worked at the college from
1912 to 1936. On the shelf to which she had
been seen reaching, there were copies of music
which dated back to the time when she had
been at the school. Most intriguing of all, was
the fact that this music teacher had died a little
before nine in the morning in the same music
building where Mrs. Buterbaugh had had her
strange experience. Mrs. Buterbaugh had seen
the ghost of the music teacher at the time of
day that she had died.

Although this incident is not a typical haunting because it was not repeated, it suggests an
idea that may be a part of other ghost reports.
Mrs. Buterbaugh felt that she actually had
been transported back in time in order to see

this particular scene. In buildings or houses that have not been changed for some time, an observer might have a similar experience without realizing that a part of the house as well as the ghost was actually the image of an earlier time.

It has been suggested that our experience of time is, in part, an illusion. Time may be a dimension similar to length and width. That is, the past and the future may have some *shape*, even though we see only the shape of the present. According to this idea, everything that existed in the past still exists. All events have shape and exist permanently. Although our consciousness must usually be concerned with the shape of the present, at times it may also notice the shape of the past.

Perhaps, then, a ghost either may take shape for an observer, or the mind of the observer himself actually may be transported to the former world of the ghost.

## THE GHOSTS THAT WERE PHOTOGRAPHED

Many interesting attempts have been made to photograph ghosts, usually without success. However, several ghosts have actually appeared on film, sometimes by accident. A now-famous photograph was taken in 1936 at a house in England called Raynham Hall, the home of Marquess and Lady Townshend. Over a period of years various residents and guests in the house had reported seeing a lady dressed in a long brown costume of the 1700's. She resembled a portrait of one of the early Townshend family members and came to be called "the brown lady."

In 1936 two professional photographers from London were taking pictures of the estate. One picture they wanted to take was that of the old oak staircase. The art director of the photographic studio, Captain Provand, had set up the camera and inserted the plate. His assistant, Indre Shira, held the lighting device as he stood behind the camera. While Captain Provand had his head beneath the black cloth at the back of the camera, his assistant suddenly noticed something coming down the stairs. He called to Captain Provand, who took the time exposure, not knowing just what it was he was shooting.

Indre Shira said he had seen a transparent veiled figure coming slowly down the steps. The captain thought it would be very unlikely that anything would show up on the film. Back at the studio later, they developed the plate in the darkroom. While the negative was in the developer they could see that there was indeed a hazy figure on the stairs. Another man, the manager of a chemical company who had an office nearby, was asked to come in to look at the negative. He saw the negative before it

Raynham Hall staircase, photographed in 1936

was taken out of the developer and placed in the fixing solution.

The final print showed a hazy-looking figure in a long costume on the stairs just as Indre Shira had seen it. The steps behind the figure showed through the image. After the picture was published, Harry Price was sent to interview the photographers. Price was an expert on trick photography, but he found no evidence of a hoax. And the men were reliable professional photographers who gave a logical account of what had happened. No one will be able to offer final proof, but the image may well be that of the brown lady often reported in Raynham Hall.

Another photograph with an unplanned ghostly subject was taken in Winchester Cathedral by the author and researcher, Hans Holzer, and published in the *Family Weekly*, March 20, 1966. Mr. Holzer had been using high-speed film to photograph locations where there were reports of ghosts. In the cathedral several figures of monks had been seen on occasions, sometimes in the aisle, sometimes in the choir loft.

On a day when no one else was inside the church, Mr. Holzer took a picture of the interior. When the photograph was developed, three hazy figures could be seen in the aisle. The photographer had not noticed anything when he shot the picture. The figures seemed unusually short, or lower than might have been expected if they were actually walking down the aisle. Some research in the church records revealed that at the time a group of monks had actually used the cathedral, the floor of the aisle had been somewhat lower. Later the floor had been raised. The images of the monks in the photograph were actually in the proper position for the floor level as it formerly had been.

In 1968 the February issue of *Fate Maga-*

*zine* contained an interesting photograph taken at the Naval College in Greenwich, London. The Reverend Ralph Hardy and his wife were touring the former palace, which was now a museum. Mr. Hardy decided to snap a photograph of the unusual spiral staircase called the Tulip Staircase. Since the stairway itself was blocked off, he took a shot looking up from one side.

Later, when the photograph was developed, a robed figure appeared in it, starting up the stairs. Part of a second figure and possibly the arm of a third could also be seen by the railing. Since Mrs. Hardy had been watching to see that all was clear, she and her husband knew there had been no one on the stairs when the picture was taken. The color film was checked by experts at a Kodak plant, who said it could not have been tampered with.

Photographs of ghosts such as these and the movie time-lapse sequence taken by NBC

cameras in Longleat manor house give strong indication of being genuine.

In order for ghosts to be photographed, there must be something existing, at least in part, in the physical world.

Rev. R. W. and Mrs. Hardy

at left, the Tulip Staircase, photographed in 1968

# SOME
# FAMOUS
# POLTERGEISTS

Poltergeist is the name used for the spirit thought to be responsible for a particular kind of disturbance, which is quite different from a haunting, but just as mystifying. A typical poltergeist case is made up of two basic kinds of events. First, objects seem to move by themselves. They may move in any variety of ways, up or down, fast or slow. The objects may be light or heavy. Occasionally the movements may damage the object or something the object strikes. People may even be struck by these flying objects. Second, there are noises, usually in the form of rappings, scrapings, knocks, thumps, or other percussive or explosive sounds. Sometimes there are noises more like those of a haunting such as footsteps.

A poltergeist disturbance usually goes on in a particular house for a period of just a few days or weeks, and then stops either gradually or suddenly. It is thought that a poltergeist occurrence may have something to do with a person living in the house. Many of the disturbances often occur near one particular family member. Unlike a haunting, the poltergeist effects occasionally follow this person to another building or home.

Usually the activity centers around a young

person in the household, often someone of preteen or early teen-age. It is as if this young family member is playing mysterious pranks on everyone, including himself. Of course, it is possible that some poltergeist cases are clever tricks played by pranksters who manage not to get caught.

But allowing for these, there are still the truly unexplained cases. They are the ones in which not only family members but witnesses outside the family report the same events. They are the cases in which the witnesses are people with educational or professional training, who are not easily deceived. In the interest of a fair investigation, they make notes of what has happened. Poltergeist activities have been carefully investigated by cautious psychical researchers, who are trained to spot trickery or exaggeration. In some of these cases, the researchers have stayed in the homes and have themselves seen and heard some of the strange events. It is because of these well-documented cases that the activities of the poltergeist are, perhaps now more than ever, worth exploring.

One of the most noticeable things about poltergeist cases is their great similarity. Cases have occurred all over the world, and those described centuries ago sound very much like the ones reported more recently. Admittedly, poltergeists do not show up very often. But over the years hundreds of examples have been collected and reviewed over and over by a whole series of psychical investigators. Even modern science cannot explain fully some of these mysterious events.

## POLTERGEISTS OF THE PAST

Perhaps one of the first well-reported poltergeist cases was that which occurred in Bingen-am-Rhein, Germany, in the year 355. Raps and knocks were heard, stones were thrown, and people were pulled out of bed. About one hundred years later a case was reported in the home of the physician to King Theodoric, of the Goths. In this one, mysterious showers of stones also occurred. A series of events reported around the year 1190 at the home of a man named William Not includes the throwing of objects and dirt and the ripping and tearing of clothes and linens.

A case that became famous was recorded in 1528 in France, in the convent of Saint Pierre de Lyon. Raps and blows were heard without any visible cause, and a strange bright light appeared for eight minutes. A report speaks of one of the nuns actually being lifted into the air invisibly. The odd happenings seemed to be connected with an eighteen-year-old girl, the first time such a connection with a young person was noted. In 1533 a group of Franciscan monks investigated strange sounds that came from the bed in which a child was sleeping. Similar raps or knocks on a bed have been reported in many later cases.

Some of the first serious research on poltergeists was done by several members of the British Society for Psychical Research. This group was formed in 1882, just a few years before a similar American organization was founded. The British society was organized to explore the kinds of unusual happenings that science could not yet explain. Among its members today are many university scholars and professional people. One of the SPR members, a teacher at Cambridge University named A.G.R. Owen, has given special attention to the study of poltergeists. As well as taking a fresh look at many past cases, Dr. Owen himself was able to investigate a case that occurred in Sauchie, Scotland, during 1960. The witnesses included a minister, three physicians, and a school teacher, as well as members of the household.

## THE SCOTTISH POLTERGEIST

Eleven-year-old Virginia Campbell and her mother had moved from Ireland to Scotland while her father stayed on in Ireland. The mother and daughter moved in with Virginia's older brother, Thomas and his wife Isabella. However, Virginia's mother took a job that prevented her from living with her daughter, so Virginia continued to stay with Thomas and Isabella and their two children.

Most of the strange happenings in this poltergeist case occurred during the last week of November. These are some of the events that were listed in the diaries kept by the witnesses. On Wednesday, November 23, Virginia was home from school. Mr. and Mrs. Campbell and Virginia were sitting in the living room. The two adults saw a sideboard move out a few inches from the wall, and then move back again. No one was near the sideboard.

That night after Virginia was in bed, loud knocks were heard all over the house. Around midnight the local minister, a Mr. Lund, was asked to come over. He discovered that the knocking was coming from the head of Virginia's bed. About the same time Mr. Lund saw a heavy linen chest raise itself slightly, move about a foot and a half, and then return to its original position.

Virginia's niece had been sleeping regularly in the same bed with Virginia. That evening the niece got out of bed during the disturbances. When she finally started to get back in bed with Virginia, loud knocks again came from the bed. Mr. Lund could feel the vibrations of the head of the bed.

On the following night, both Mr. Lund and Dr. Nisbet, a physician, were present in Virginia's bedroom and reported further happenings. Virginia was in bed and her head was on the pillow. The pillow was seen to rotate itself about one third of a turn. Again there were knockings and the linen chest rocked back and forth. Also an odd rippling motion passed over the exposed surface of the pillow. .

On Friday Virginia stayed home in the morning, but went to school in the afternoon. Her teacher saw the lid of Virginia's desk rise by itself several times. An empty desk behind Virginia raised itself about an inch off the floor and settled down in a new position. The teacher checked the desk, but found nothing that could have caused the movement.

Incidents like these were observed and reported every day for more than a week. The same incidents occurred several times over. Once at school Virginia came up to ask the teacher a question. As she stood near the teacher's desk with her hands behind her back, a blackboard pointer began to jiggle and rolled off the desk. Then the desk itself began to vibrate, and one end swung around into a new position.

In Virginia's bedroom the knocks continued at night, and the strange rippling effect was seen on the covers as well as the pillow. The rotation of the pillow occurred several more times. Even when Virginia could be seen lying quietly, the mysterious events continued. Finally two physicians, Dr. Nisbet and Dr. Logan, decided to take a movie camera and a tape recorder into the bedroom. Although the strange rippling waves again were seen to pass over the bed covers that night, the camera could not be started quickly enough to capture them. However, for about an hour the tape recorder picked up the poltergeist noises including the knockings and a sound of sawing or rasping.

Afterward the happenings were less bothersome and little more was reported. However, the tape recording was saved. It was later played on the air during a special radio program about the case prepared by the British Broadcasting Corporation.

## THE FARM POLTERGEIST

Just a few years before the case in Scotland, several poltergeist incidents in the United States were reported in the newspapers. One of them happened near Hartville, Missouri, on the farm of Mr. and Mrs. Clinton Ward. A newspaper article about the case reached the Parapsychology Laboratory of Duke University, located in Durham, North Carolina. A researcher from the laboratory, William Cox, took a trip to the farm to investigate the reports. The happenings seemed to have something to do with Betty Ruth, the nine-year-old daughter of the Wards.

It all began when Betty Ruth was cracking walnuts at her grandmother's house. Suddenly both Betty and her grandmother were surrounded with walnuts floating and hopping around the room. The nuts bounced to the ceiling as if made of rubber. Some of them seemed to roll gently down the curtains. Betty's grandmother was struck several times by the flying nuts, and one almost broke her glasses.

Betty Ruth and her grandmother went to Betty's house to tell the rest of the family about the strange events. As soon as they got there, buckets, bowls, and other objects began to move around the house by themselves. After a few days, during which this activity continued,

Suddenly the room was full of flying walnuts.

Mr. Cox arrived at the Wards' home. With him was a young assistant named Jim Bethel, who had a tape recorder. The second day that Mr. Cox and Mr. Bethel were on the scene, events began to occur while they were in the house. A can of shoe polish seemed to come out of nowhere and hit Mr. Bethel on the foot. Soon a small rock fell down beside Betty while she was sitting on the sofa with her hands together. Mr. Cox watched a walnut fall onto a nearby table.

A short time later the observers were standing in the kitchen. Betty's grandmother was telling of an earlier event. A stewpot had lifted itself from the stove and had floated into a bedroom where it spilled the stew on the floor. As Mr. Cox followed Betty and her grandmother through the kitchen, he heard a table move although no one was near it. Suddenly as Mr. Cox passed a chair, a heavy oil lantern that was on it tipped over. It had been resting squarely on

the chair, and no one had touched either the chair or the lantern. Betty was six feet away. Then as Mr. Bethel approached a water cooler both he and Mr. Cox clearly saw a bar of dry soap jump from a nearby table to the floor. Later, while sitting in another room, Mr. Cox was hit by small pieces of bark that seemed to come from nowhere.

The Hartville case is one of the few in which various poltergeist activities occurred while the investigator was present. Mr. Cox did not have to rely on the reports of other witnesses. He had seen some of the events clearly himself and found in them no evidence of trickery or any other natural explanation.

A number of the incidents of the case involved heavy objects. The Wards' older daughter, Lola Mae, had been washing clothes on the porch. A tub of wet laundry flew off the porch, spilling the clean clothes on the ground. Five people, including a visitor, saw this accident happen. Once Mrs. Ward was sitting on a bed and while others watched, the head end of the bed rose more than a foot off the floor. Two more times the bed rose and fell, lifting Mrs. Ward with it. Before it came down the last time, Mrs. Ward slid off and it settled gently to the floor.

One of the most curious incidents happened away from the house. Betty Ruth and two of her brothers had gone shopping in Lebanon, a nearby town, with their mother. As they walked

down the aisle of a clothing store, a pair of shoes flew through the air and landed between Betty Ruth and her mother. They landed perfectly lined up with the heels toward Betty Ruth. A clerk saw the flight of the shoes as well as the Ward family.

At the close of his investigation Mr. Cox reported that many of the events went beyond the limits of "ordinary fraud." He interviewed a large number of the witnesses, but no simple physical explanations could be found for most of the disturbances.

However, many of the incidents did seem to center around Betty Ruth. If in some unknown way emotional energy could cause the strange events it must be at the unconscious level. Whenever the subconscious mind expresses itself, it is likely to do so symbolically, and the symbols must be interpreted, as those in dreams are. For instance, the laundry tub incident, the can of shoe polish, and the bar of soap near the water cooler all could symbolize the idea of cleaning. The objects might suggest the need for a "cleanup" in a situation or attitudes.

Developing this word-symbol idea leads to other interesting possibilities:

Walnuts flying around the room might mean,

"This place is full of 'nuts.' " The overturned stewpot could be interpreted as meaning, "Things are in a 'real stew' now." The incident in which the oil lantern tipped over near the investigator could be an attempt to say, "How about 'throwing some light' on things?"

These particular interpretations are just guesses, of course. But they are in keeping with knowledge of the way in which the subconscious mind expresses thoughts. If the events are really a sort of coded message, they may begin to make sense and the idea behind them can be figured out.

## THE BOTTLE-POPPING MYSTERY

A poltergeist case somewhat similar to that of the Wards took place in a home on Long Island. It also was thoroughly investigated. Early in 1958 newspaper reports of the case alerted the staff of the Parapsychology Laboratory of

Duke University. The disturbances occurred in the home of Mr. and Mrs. James Herrmann and their two children, thirteen-year-old Lucille and twelve-year-old James. Local police had looked into the events but found no explanation. Two investigators from the Duke laboratory, J. G. Pratt and William Roll, arranged to go to Long Island to study the case. The records of the police and the Duke investigators combine to make an unusually clear report of the events. The two Duke researchers later published a long summary of the case in the *Journal of Parapsychology*.

The strange events in the household began on February 3 and continued until March 10. They started when James came home from school on Monday and found that a ceramic doll and a ship model in his room were both broken. They were on top of a dresser, and it almost looked as though the doll had struck the ship. Later the same day strange noises were heard. In various rooms several bottles were found to have opened and spilled. In the master bedroom a bottle of holy water was found uncapped and spilled. At the same time bottles of shampoo and Kaopectate in the bathroom had lost their caps, tipped over, and spilled. A bottle of starch was found spilled under the kitchen sink, and in the basement James and Mrs. Herrmann saw a bleach bottle smash on the floor after jumping from a cardboard box. On Thursday two bottles in the bathroom lost their caps and spilled. On Friday a bottle of ammonia under the kitchen sink behaved the same way. On several occasions wine bottles were found overturned.

Mr. Herrmann felt at first that the events were just pranks. But on Sunday the bottles were tipping again. While the family was in the dining room they all heard noises coming from several other rooms. When they checked they found that the holy water was spilled once more. The starch in the kitchen was also found running out of the bottle. No one had been in these rooms until the noises were heard, but later the same day Mr. Herrmann was standing in the bathroom doorway watching James brush his teeth. As he glanced at the vanity table he saw the shampoo bottle and the Kaopectate bottle slide in different directions and fall off the table.

Mr. Herrmann was now convinced that more than simple pranks were occurring in his house. He called the police, who sent men to interview the family and to search out the cause of the disturbances. A detective was then assigned full time to cover the case. As the bottle spilling continued, along with movements of furniture and other objects, the police tested every possible cause for the events. An oscillograph for measuring minute vibrations was placed in the basement. No unusual vibrations were recorded, although a number of events occurred while the oscillograph was in the house.

Some of the liquids that had spilled were analyzed at the police laboratory. No unusual contents were found. The lighting company checked the house and ground wiring and fuses. Everything about the wiring was normal. The detective working on the case went over the household appliances for vibrations, and a cap was put on the chimney to stop any downdrafts.

College staff engineers were called to examine the house. A local building department tested for settling. Maps were studied to see if there were any underground streams near the house. There were none. RCA engineers checked the area around the house for radio frequencies and found nothing unusual. The plumbing was inspected for vibrations that might carry through the house. And the flight schedule of a nearby airfield was consulted for any correspondence between the noises of plane takeoffs and events in the house, but none was found.

No scientist or specialist could find any

logical physical explanation for the unusual happenings in the house. The police department found the "bottle-popping mystery" as strange as it was in the beginning. And as the weeks went by more items other than bottles were reported moving around in the house.

Several times the porcelain figurines of a man and a woman were seen to fly off the end table in the living room. Finally they broke and shattered. A ceramic figurine of the Virgin

Mary flew across the master bedroom and struck a mirror. In James's room the disturbances became violent. Pieces of heavy bedroom furniture moved or fell over, some several times. Once the globe in James's room was found in the middle of his bed. Another time James's room was empty and the door was open. The globe rolled out of the room and stopped at the foot of a guest, who was seated in the living room.

By the time the disturbances in the Herrmann house stopped, there had occurred a total of sixty-seven events according to the report of the Duke investigators. Five of the strange happenings had taken place while one or both of the Duke staff members were in the house. Their report included diagrams of the first-floor and basement levels of the Herrmann house. All of the objects that moved were located on the charts, and lines with arrows showed the direction and the distance each object had traveled.

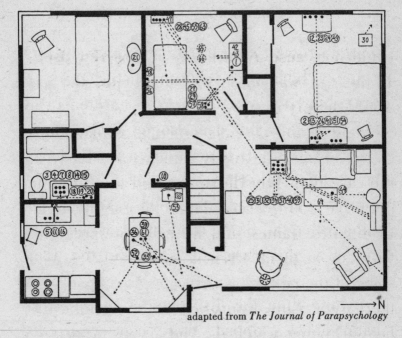

adapted from *The Journal of Parapsychology*

In this diagram of the "bottle-popping" case
the events have been numbered. Black dots
represent small objects, and dotted lines
show the directions in which objects moved.

The Duke investigators tried to discover
ways in which the strange poltergeist activities
could be duplicated. They experimented with
chemicals added to the liquids inside bottles
like those which had opened in the Herrmann
home. Chemicals could cause gas inside to ex-
pand and explode the bottles. But such pressure

could not cause a bottle cap to unscrew itself. If the cap was loose to begin with, the gas would simply escape.

None of the possible practical explanations of the events was really satisfactory. Early in the case both Mr. Herrmann and the full-time detective had accused James of rigging practical jokes. James said he had nothing to do with any of them. Even if James had managed some of the poltergeist effects through trickery, there were many events that had occurred while he was being watched. And it was even less likely that the Herrmann family, the police, and the psychical investigators had all decided to make up the whole story.

In the typical poltergeist pattern the activities in the Herrmann house were centered around a young person. There are similarities between this case and that of the Wards. Perhaps, as it might have happened with Betty Ruth, young James was unconsciously broadcasting an important message. Many of the

events in the Herrmann household follow the same cleaning-up theme that was suggested in the case of Betty Ruth Ward. Most of the tipped-over bottles contained a liquid that had something to do with cleanliness. Bleach and ammonia are household cleaning liquids. Shampoo and cologne are for personal use and Kaopectate is for internal disorders. Holy water is a symbol of that which is clean and pure in a spiritual way, and wine is a sacramental symbol. Perhaps again the message might be,

"There needs to be a complete 'cleanup' in attitudes around here."

One researcher suggested that the bottle poppings might also symbolize the expression "blowing your top," a common word pun.

In a similar way the incidents involving the movements of James's globe might be a way of saying, "Won't you please take a look at James's world?" The breaking of the male and female figurines might suggest James's attempt to attract the attention of his parents, and hidden anger toward them as well.

Whatever explanation is attempted, the evidence is strong that something not yet fully understood was at work in this mysterious "bottle-popping" case.

## THE STORE POLTERGEIST

The same investigators, J. G. Pratt and William Roll, who had worked on the Herrmann case, made a study of a somewhat different poltergeist incident in Miami, Florida. The disturbances were taking place at a wholesale novelty company, and again the local police had been unable to find a solution to the mystery. William Roll, at the time representing the Psychical Research Foundation, spent ten days observing events at the store. Altogether, during that time, more than 150 glasses and novelty gadgets fell or flew from the shelves and crashed to the floor. All of the activity was in the vicinity of a nineteen-year-old shipping clerk. Most of the flying articles seemed to move behind the clerk in a counterclockwise direction. More objects fell from the shelves closer to the clerk and fewer objects fell farther away. The movements suggested a sort of invisible whirlpool with the clerk at the center.

The clerk agreed to go to the Psychical Research Foundation for some tests. Results suggested that he felt hostile to the owners of the business, but was not free to express this feeling openly. The clerk also was given tests with laboratory devices called PK machines. PK

The clerk seemed surrounded by a whirlpool of energy, which decreased with distance.

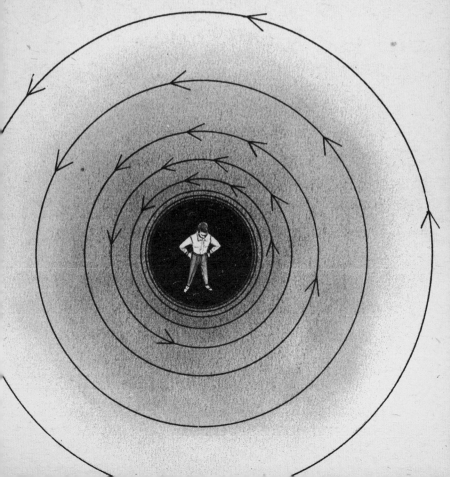

stands for psychokinesis. "Psycho" means "of the mind" and "kinesis" means "motion." Psychokinesis is the term for the idea of mind over matter, and PK is its abbreviation.

The PK machines are simply devices for shaking and rolling dice. The person being tested tries to concentrate on the way in which he would like the dice to fall. The Miami clerk did score somewhat better than chance would permit in the laboratory test. A test result like his suggests that the person can influence the movement of the dice without touching them. But more remarkably, while he was there, several of the objects in the room moved unnaturally as the items had moved in the Miami store. A large lamp fell from a table ten feet away, and the bottom of the electric dice tumbling cage fell out several times.

# EXPLAINING GHOSTS AND POLTERGEISTS

It is no longer enough to ask whether ghosts and poltergeists are real. Evidently at least some of these occurrences are genuine and reveal to us an aspect of man and the universe that we do not yet understand. The better question to ask now is what is the nature of the unusual phases of reality demonstrated by ghosts and poltergeists?

## MEMORIES IN SPACE

Physicists and mathematicians are aware that reality is much "larger" than was formerly supposed. Space seems to have dimensions beyond the length, width, and depth with which we are familiar. Some investigators theorize that living people affect the space around themselves and objects in that space through these unknown dimensions. Houses and furniture may contain impressions of events that have occurred in the past. When ghosts appear, these memories of past occurrences are being played back like old phonograph recordings or movies. This suggestion is in keeping with the observation that the actions of most ghosts resemble sleepwalkers going through a familiar routine.

## SEPARATION OF CONSCIOUSNESS

In addition to the newly suspected greater dimensions of space, another idea that can help to explain ghosts is that an individual's consciousness may be able to separate from his body.

In some of the attempts to investigate haunted houses, sensitives or mediums have been used to attempt to communicate with former residents who have died. In order for this communication to take place, the consciousness of the dead person apparently would have to exist separately from his body and continue to exist after his death. In a few cases information obtained in this way has been found accurate.

The occurrence of ghosts of the living also seems to indicate the possibility of this separation. A case is reported of an English woman who had dreams at night that she was walking around in the rooms of an old country house. Later she and her husband arranged to spend the summer at a large estate called Ballachulish, in Scotland. The man made all the arrangements for the visit; his wife had never seen the place. When she arrived she knew the house immediately as the one in her dreams. At the door the owner of the estate gave her a startled look. She learned later that she was recognized as a ghost that had been seen moving around the rooms of the house. The owners were now meeting the ghost, in the flesh. And she was able to describe the appearance of all the rooms even before she was taken into them!

A common kind of ghost, the one seen at the moment a friend or relative dies, may well be another form of this phenomenon of separation. In the files of the psychic-research organizations there are hundreds of reports of such appearances. Either during the day or at night a person suddenly sees a relative, who lives a good distance away, in the room with him. Sometimes the individual thinks the relative has actually come to visit. The relative may speak briefly, usually a message of encouragement or reassurance. Then the ghost disappears. Several hours later the person who saw the ghost receives news of the death of that person.

Studies of such cases as these suggest that separation of consciousness may take place temporarily during the life of the body and, it seems probable, permanently at death. In other words, a person may have a sort of invisible but real existence that either overlaps with the ordinary physical body or can exist separately. When the invisible existence has separated from the body but overlaps with ordinary space, it creates a structure that may be seen— what we call a ghost.

## ENERGY OF THE MIND

Consciousness also may be able to express itself in other unusual ways. Some individuals seem to be able to transfer emotional energy to objects and actually cause them to move.

The poltergeist may simply be a very extreme example of the transfer of mental and emotional energy from one source to another. If it is a case of mind over matter, we might expect the definite link with a single personality that is common in poltergeist cases and also with PK experiments in the laboratory. In the case of Virginia Campbell, movements of objects occurred around the girl even when she was at school. And in the case on the Missouri farm, the disturbances followed Betty Ruth from her grandmother's house to her own home.

If a young person is really emotionally responsible for the poltergeist effects, how does this phenomenon work? Psychologists suggest that the answer is in some way connected with the changes a young person goes through in becoming an adult. These changes are so great that they present real problems to many young people, but they often do not want to talk about them. Also, most adolescents have an unusual amount of energy. If enough channels for using the energy are found, there is no trouble. However, sometimes this energy is trapped inside the adolescent along with his bottled-up feelings. The poltergeist may be a channel for this trapped energy. In the case in the Miami store, the young clerk did not like his bosses, but he was not free to tell them so. Perhaps, unknown even to the boy, his hostile energy actually caused the objects to fly off the shelves. In the case in Scotland, the young Irish girl found herself in a strange household without either of her parents. Suddenly she had to live in close contact with other children just at the time when she most needed privacy. Like the young clerk, she too was reluctant to express her hurts and fears openly.

Reports have noted that some of the objects involved in poltergeist cases were not in the rooms to begin with. For instance, stones have been seen to fall in enclosed rooms with no apparent means of entry. If objects actually can pass through other objects, this phenomenon is further evidence, not just of the possibilities of mind over matter, but that true space includes dimensions beyond those which we commonly know.

The ghosts of haunted houses and the pranks of poltergeists are fascinating subjects for study and speculation. Perhaps, also, they actually can give us clues to the nature of a larger reality than we ordinarily experience in our daily lives.

## ABOUT THE AUTHOR

Larry Kettelkamp was born in Harvey, Illinois, and graduated from the University of Illinois, receiving a B.F.A. degree in painting in 1953. The following year he studied illustration at the Pratt Institute, Brooklyn, New York.

After two years' service as a lieutenant in the Army Mr. Kettelkamp returned to Urbana, Illinois, where he joined the staff of Spencer Press. Now he and his family live in New Jersey, and he devotes his time to free-lance writing, illustrating, and designing.

Larry Kettelkamp's first book, *Magic Made Easy*, grew out of a lifelong hobby. He also plays the piano, the classical guitar, and the recorder, and many of his books reflect his strong interest in music. When the author is considering a new book, he often discusses the project with his children and finds their interests helpful to him in developing his subject.